GOD'S
Passionate
DESIRE

... for unity in the church!

To David —

PAUL BERSCHE

Jn 17:21-23

Copyright © 2013 by PAUL BERSCHE

GOD'S PASSIONATE DESIRE... for unity in the church!
by PAUL BERSCHE

Printed in the United States of America

ISBN 9781625095664

All rights reserved solely by the author. The author guarantees all contents are original and do not infringe upon the legal rights of any other person or work. No part of this book may be reproduced in any form without the permission of the author. The views expressed in this book are not necessarily those of the publisher.

Unless otherwise indicated, Bible quotations are taken from The Holy Bible, New Living Translation. Copyright © 2007 by The Tyndale House Foundation.

www.xulonpress.com

CONTENTS

ACKNOWLEDGEMENTS vii

WRITING STYLE AND TERMS ix

INTRODUCTION xiii

CHAPTER ONE: BEGINNING UNITY 21

CHAPTER TWO: ONENESS UNITY 29

CHAPTER THREE: SPIRIT UNITY 39

CHAPTER FOUR: FAITH UNITY 49

CHAPTER FIVE: UNITY MODEL—THE
                 MOST IMPORTANT THING! 57

CHAPTER SIX: INTENTIONAL UNITY 69

EPILOGUE 77

ACKNOWLEDGEMENTS

Carolyn
My first and only love. My Bride, my partner, friend, and personal intercessor for fifty-six years of marriage and ministry. She is steadfast, unmovable, and always abounding in the love of God. We press on!!

G. J. Bersche
My natural and spiritual father. I learned sonship, servanthood, and submission from his instruction and example. My deep love for The Father and His Church flowed from Dad's heart.

WRITING STYLE AND TERMS

*P*lease note that all references to God, His Son Jesus Christ, and the Holy Spirit, including personal pronouns, are capitalized. I chose to specifically acknowledge the final sovereignty and authority of the only true God in this unique manner, even to the point of violating grammatical rules.

In like manner, I have chosen to never acknowledge satan or his related names, as in any way to be construed as equal to Almighty God. Therefore, I do not capitalize his name(s), even to the point of violating grammatical rules.

I have, in addition, chosen to capitalize "The Church" to undeniably identify that every born-again Christian worldwide, finally and ultimately belongs only to Jesus Christ, the Son of the Living God. All born-again Christians, His people, are His Church and His Bride. Therefore, "The Church."

The "Bride-Church" or "Church-Bride" is my effort to establish the clear recognition that "The Church" is indeed the promised and anticipated Bride of Jesus Christ. Which way and when those hyphenated words appear in the text is determined by the context: Bride-Church when the context is the bride, and vice versa.

I have used the term "the church," lower case, to reference the difference between born-again Christians worldwide, who are "The Church," and those who are born again in local church congregations around the world.

"The Body of Christ" is a reference to the biblical fact that "The Church" is the living representation of Jesus Christ on the earth. He is the Head of His Church, and we are His Body on the earth. We are therefore, the expression of Who He is ". . . on earth, as it is in heaven."

Godhead Unity, refers to the interpersonal relationship of the Holy Trinity, God the Father, the Son, and the Holy Spirit. It is an endeavor to encourage a better understanding of God's definition of the specific kind of Unity He so passionately desires The Church to demonstrate to an unbelieving world. He longs for us to want to "become one as He is one." (John 17:21)

Unity and One or Oneness
1. Biblical words purposely used by John and Paul to differentiate from any other kind of perceived unity in the world. They reflect the concept of one corporate unit recognized as one of a kind, with no divided parts.
2. Totally "other" with no mixture. This unity then is more than mere sentimental unanimity. It is the living reality of the Holy Spirit uniting Christians in the Holy Spirit.

3. It further declares there are no gradations in this unity, that is, no great Christians in comparison to lesser Christians. Though there are levels of maturity, they are not to be misconstrued to possess a greater or lesser value to their fellow believers. This unity has no place for comparison or competition.

The "Bride-Church" or "Church-Bride" is my effort to establish the clear recognition that "The Church" is indeed the promised and anticipated Bride of Jesus Christ.

Finally, I have used an abundance of scriptural references to strengthen the message of the imperative necessity God has placed on the unity of The Church. My desire is the reader will capture the urgency and the passion for the need for the truth of the unity of The Church, and do something about it in his/her own life and sphere of influence. Though personal real-life experiences are interesting, I didn't want anything, no matter how appealing, to distract us from becoming willing captives of the divine imperative of unity in The Church! It is not an option! Therefore, I strongly encourage you to at least read the scriptures printed on the chapter introduction pages. Thank you, and may the reading of the living Word of God challenge your mind and heart and give you His passion for unity in The Church.

Italics—wherever italics occur, they are my addition for the sake of emphasis.

GOD'S PASSIONATE DESIRE... for unity in the church!

*"I don't want any of you sitting around on your
hands. I don't want anyone strolling off;
down some path that goes nowhere. And mark
that you do this with humility and discipline–
not in fits and starts, but steadily, pouring yourselves
out for each other in acts of love, alert at noticing
differences and quick at mending fences.
You were all called to travel on the same road
and in the same direction, so stay together,
both outwardly and inwardly. You have
one Master, one faith, one baptism, one God and
Father of all, who rules over all, works through
all, and is present in all. Everything you
are and think and do is permeated with Oneness.
But that doesn't mean you should all look and speak
and act the same. Out of the generosity of
Christ, each of us is given his own gift.*

*He handed out gifts, above and below, filled
heaven with his gifts, filled earth with his
gifts. He handed out gifts of apostle, prophet,
evangelist, and pastor-teacher to train
Christians in skilled servant work, working with
Christ's body, the church, until we're all
moving rhythmically and easily with each other,
efficient and graceful in response to God's Son,
fully mature adults, fully developed within
and without, fully alive like Christ."*

Ephesians 4:2–13 MSG

INTRODUCTION

This book was born out of more than fifty-five years of ministry. It is not meant to be a scholarly presentation. That is a task for someone much more qualified. My purpose is to try to provide a revealing look at The Church Jesus so passionately prayed for in John 17, and contrast that with the one we appear to have endorsed as a good-enough-for-now alternative.

This book was born out of real-life experience. My father's fifty years of pastoral experience and passionate commitment to initiate and coordinate unity in his local church, along with the pastors of his city, prepared me to say "yes" when God called me to follow in Dad's footsteps. It was ten years after I had begun pastoring when the Holy Spirit of God planted an unexpected but inescapable passion in my heart for the unity of His Church. That was forty-five years ago. That passion for His Church-Bride lives on in me with ever-increasing intensity.

This book was born out of what I call "Heart-Stuff." It's not definable in academic terms. It can only be defined in

Holy Spirit-life terms[1]. You know, terms that live and breathe with both knowledge and feeling: words like disciple, father, conviction, commitment, and passion. Passion—now there is a "Heart-Stuff" word! It evokes fervor, affection, excitement, compelling action, and sacrifice! Those with passion are willing to suffer and die, if necessary, for the object of their passion. God just needs a few more good men who are, from the inside-out, made of "Heart-Stuff."

By the way, "Heart-Stuff" happens inside when your conscience[2] is clear, your mind[3] is set on Jesus, your will[4] is surrendered to His, and your emotions[5] are released to freely express your passion for God and His ways. Actually, "Heart-Stuff" is better illustrated in Jesus's high priestly prayer. I know this is difficult, especially when you know a passage very well, but do your best to read it as though this is your first time seeing it! Listen for His heartbeat for His soon-to-be-born Church.

> "My prayer is not for the world, but for those you have given me, because they belong to you. Now I am departing from the world; they are staying in this world, but I am coming to you. Holy Father, you have given me your name; now protect them by the power of your name so that

---

[1] John 14:26 NLT
[2] Acts 23:1 NLT; I Timothy 3:9 NLT
[3] Colossians 3:2 NLT
[4] Mark 3:35 NLT
[5] Galatians 5:22,23 NLT

INTRODUCTION

they will be united just as we are.
I have given them your word. And the world
hates them because they do not belong to the
the world, just as I do not belong to the world.
They do not belong to this world any more than I do.
I am praying not only for these disciples but also
for all who will ever believe in me through their
message. I pray that they will all be one, just as
you and I are one—as you are in me, Father, and I
am in you. And may they be in us so that the
world will believe you sent me. I have given
them the glory you gave me, so they may be one as
we are one. I am in them and you are in me.
May they experience such perfect unity that the
world will know that you sent me and that you
love them as much as you love me.
O righteous Father, the world doesn't know you,
but I do; and these disciples know you sent me. I
have revealed you to them, and I will continue
to do so. Then your love for me will be in them,
and I will be in them.
John 17:9, 11, 14, 16–17, 20–25 NLT

Did you feel His passion? Do you get a sense of His personal love, reaching from that present moment to the vision He had for the future in His eternal Church?[6] Do you capture the imperative in His intercession—that ". . . just as we are

---

[6] John 17:20; Acts 2:39; Psalm 71 & 78 NLT

one . . ."[7] is not merely an option for His Church? Oneness is such a mandate for Him that He has been interceding and continues to intercede for us until we mature enough to deliberately choose to unify as His Church-Bride—now.[8]

Almost in desperation, He prays to possess for Himself a Church that will be the realization of His intercessory vision in John 17. He wants it to be like the one He was planning to birth in Acts chapter 2! From the "Heart-Stuff" disciples He prayed with and taught[9] for three years, to the words He chose, "one" and "unity," to define her, Jesus made it clear the kind of Church He wants to be His Bride. Only one kind will be acceptable!

Given that The Church is the place where God lives, the people of God have a mandate—an imperative—to live together as one.[10] That oneness-unity is His divine covenant with His Church and our covenant with Him. Choosing to make it an option is sin. Protecting "our kind" of Christians and Church, by minimizing relationships with other Christians, is separatism and exclusivism that leads to division, suspicion, and lack of trust in one another. It is sin!

Fifty-six years ago my bride and I signed our marriage license. It was a valid legal document intended to seal our life time contract to love one another, "til death do us part."

However, for us it was more than a contract; it was a

---

[7] John 17:21 NLT
[8] Hebrews 7:25 NLT
[9] John 13–21; Acts 2:47 NLT
[10] 1Corinthians 3:16–17 NLT

INTRODUCTION

covenant. Our marriage contract was merely a legal challenge. The difference between a contract and a covenant is this: a contract is conditional. It says, "I will . . . if." The condition is that if you fulfill your part, I will fulfill my part, and . . . by the way, from now on, I am the judge of your success rate. On the other hand, a covenant makes a straight forward commitment. A covenant says, "I will!" It is unconditional! In effect, it says, "No matter what you say or do, no matter who you become—there are no conditions. I will love you!" You see, it is not merely unkind, or "not nice" of me to not keep my covenant with my wife; it is sin.

That is Jesus's covenant with us when we were born of the Spirit. It is that same covenant He prays we will keep with "one another" in the body of Christ. God's kind of oneness requires a sacrificial "covenant marriage" mindset toward His Son and His Church. To not obey this imperative is to sin against the will and purposes of God. Simply said, He desires things to be "on earth as it is in heaven."[11]

The Holy Spirit continues to use the following two verses of scripture to keep my life aware of His purpose for us on the earth today.[12]

> "Please, just for a moment. The thing that has me so upset is that I care about you so much—this is the passion of God burning inside me! I promised your hand in marriage to Christ, presented you as

---

[11] Matthew 6:10 NLT
[12] 2 Corinthians 3:16,17 NLT

a pure virgin to her husband. And now I'm afraid that exactly as the snake seduced Eve with his smooth patter, you are being lured away from the simple purity of your love for Christ."
2 Corinthians 11:2, 3 MSG

This is the passion of my heart, The Church living in the oneness unity Jesus prayed for. The little phrase "simple purity" means "single minded and exclusive" devotion to Jesus. When that is the way we "live and move and exist,"[13] then the rebellion and resistance, excuses and lies of disunity, will be seen for what they are—sin against God and one another. When you love Him, you love what He loves! Therefore, how can we, with integrity, substitute a grudging tolerance for fellow believers and churches and still call it the authentic love of God? He loved your uncooperative intolerant self into oneness with Him and called you and me to the same with other resisters in the body of Christ.

At the risk of sounding presumptuous, it is my love for Him and His Church that is the foundation for my personal forthrightness, and application of this book to our lives and relationships, with Jesus and His beloved Church. Whether Jesus is returning sooner or later, The Church must no longer tolerate "Christian political correctness," or . . . the fear of offending a favored saint, . . . or a famous Christian leader, or operate in mild-mannered waffling, while we delay obeying

---

[13] Acts 17:29 NLT

INTRODUCTION

Jesus's divine imperative for His Church! I fear most of us live in contract mode with Jesus, and one another.

This book is not intended to be the final word on unity in The Church. It has been my hope to write from my heart to your heart. However, I do confess I did plan to strongly remind and challenge us to allow the Holy Spirit to teach us His ways, and deeply convict us of what we "old timers" used to call "the exceeding sinfulness of sin."[14] At all costs to ourselves, we must, individually and corporately, take deliberate, intentional, and even sacrificial action steps to become the fulfillment of Jesus's Passionate Desire . . . for unity in The Church! I invite you to join me on this journey of hope!

Paul Bersche
Farmington Hills, Michigan

---

[14] Romans 7:13 NLT

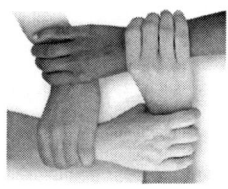

CHAPTER ONE

BEGINNING UNITY

"We look at the Son and see the God who cannot be seen. We look at the Son and see God's original purpose in everything created. For everything, absolutely everything, above and below, visible and invisible, rank after rank after rank of angels—everything, got started in him and finds its purpose in him. He was there before any of it came into existence and holds it all together right up to this moment. And when it comes to the church, he organizes and holds it together, like a head does a body. He was supreme in the beginning and—leading the resurrection parade—he is supreme in the end. From beginning to end he's there, towering far above everything, everyone. So spacious is he, so roomy, that everything of God finds its proper place in him without crowding. Not only that, but all the broken and dislocated pieces of the universe—people and things, animals and atoms—get properly fixed and

fit together in vibrant harmonies, all because of his death, his blood that poured down from the Cross."
Colossians 1:15–20 MSG

"In the beginning God created the heavens and the earth. And the earth was formless and void, and darkness was over the surface of the deep; and the Spirit of God was moving over the surface of the waters."
Genesis 1:1, 2 NLT

*F*irst, there is God! Only God: God the Father, the Son, and the Holy Spirit. Everywhere God is, there is the full expression of the radiant and awesome glory of the Oneness of Himself! Our God doesn't do acts of unity; He is unity! In fact, unity is not merely a great idea God had one day. It is that in the glorious splendor of Himself, Unity stood on the precipice of nothingness, in the overshadowing cloud of His Presence, simultaneously conceiving and creating all things, after their kind and in His image.[15] This is just the beginning expression of the ongoing mystery of the majesty of our God!

There is something of great significance here. Established in eternity past, it has set in motion the pattern for the creative lifestyle of mankind until Jesus comes again! Notice that unity requires and releases order, and order is reflective of unity. The prioritized and sequential order of all creation illustrates this. Standing in His sovereign authority, the Godhead, unity Himself, spoke order to the chaos of useless

---

[15] Genesis 1:26, 27; 2:7 NLT

and empty formlessness. As He spoke, the anointing flowed from unity, and immediately each created thing[16] began to competently operate in its ultimate and most mature intention. Of course they did and do. The divine order of sovereignty, authority, unity, order, anointing, and government was released for the efficiency and effectiveness of the operation of mankind upon the earth.

That mysterious sounding word, *anointing*, simply means the God-given ability to cause the supernatural to be received as though it were a natural and normal order of life. To maintain and sustain this divine operational pattern, God appointed mankind to "fill the earth and govern it . . ."

Everything that was made is from Him, for Him, and to Him.[17] It all accommodates Him and His purpose. He so desires fellowship and relationship that He made man in His own image and likeness. From the time of Adam and Eve man has continued to find ways to break this relationship with God. Like people in all times of history, they just couldn't sustain their relationship with God because they chose to not pay the price of maintaining it! Like the patterns of the Israelites, there were periods of unity and miraculous blessing, but their faithfulness to God was always distracted by what they saw to be a better offer. Despite our history, God loves us so much that He continues to provide ways for man to be restored to that unity with Him. Even now, the blood of the cross continues to be available for us to be redeemed and restored to

---

[16] Genesis 1:28 NLT
[17] Colossians 1:16 NLT

GOD'S PASSIONATE DESIRE... for unity in the church!

our relationship with Jesus Christ.[18] Why? He desires us to be one with Him.[19]

Whether we realize it or not, The Church dominates history and will dominate all future world events, until Jesus Christ comes again. When He comes, He will come to receive the Bride His Father sent Him to possess after He had created all things in heaven and earth! This is what Jesus so fervently prayed for: "I gave them the glory You gave Me, so they (church) may be *one as we are one* I am in them and You are in Me. May they experience such perfect unity *that the world will know* that you sent Me and that You love them as much as You love Me."[20] How was He going to possess His Bride? Through a powerful and irresistibly unified and loving church. Biblically and historically people became Christ followers because they experienced the corporate impact, influence, and impartation of the overwhelming feeling and healing of God's love that flows like rivers of living water[21] from the combined weight of the testimony of caring lives.

This powerfully profound unity, unfortunately, is the one method of worldwide evangelism we have only rarely employed. God created us to be one church, led by and living for "one Lord, one faith, one baptism, and one God and Father, who is over all and in all and living through all."[22] He is satisfied with His plan for one reason, that the world

---

[18] Colossians 1:18–21; Philippians 2:6–8 NLT
[19] 1 Peter 1:18–20; Romans 5:8–11 NLT
[20] John 17:22–23 NLT
[21] John 7:37–39 NLT
[22] Ephesians 4:5–6 NLT

will know that God loves them as much as He loves His Son, Jesus! His passionate desire is that the whole world will experience The Church—His Body—whoever they are and wherever they live, as one and the same!

Here is a truth we Christian church folks have overlooked. God is *One!* We are not! He created us to be one. Passionately and patiently He prayed and led us to be one. He has given us Biblical examples of the power and effectiveness of unity. So it is not an option. However, we have proven we believe we have a better plan, and it doesn't include the sacrifice required to be one—with Him or one another. We seem to fear that to experience ourselves as one and the same wouldn't allow us to enjoy our own identity and uniqueness. However, in God's plan, He thinks being in unity with Him and one another is supernaturally unique. Additionally, if you are looking for radical, "unreal," and mind-boggling ways for reaching a sin-scattered world, He believes The Church living ". . . in harmony with each other . . . with no divisions . . . of one mind, united in thought and purpose . . . and not quarreling . . ."[23] with one another is a powerful testimony of "unique and crazy unreal." God's simple oneness unity plan works, because for Him, a community whose Bible-believing churches are recognized as one and the same by the way they corporately minister over the long haul, not just occasional community projects, establishes their credibility. This breaks the power of their resistance, enabling them to experience the radical, unique, and unreal power of "the word of their

---

[23] I Corinthians 1:10 NLT

testimony."[24]

The hard-to-take truth is God is Unity. He created all things to exist efficiently and effectively in unity. Sin destroys unity. God made, and continues to make, provision for man to be redeemed and reconciled to Him and one another. To Him it is imperative that we are one just as He is one. Therefore, every church congregation and their leaders are either working together with Him for the unity of The Church, or they are unintentionally working together with satan to keep The Church ineffective, mediocre, divided and destroyed.

God created *all things* to express Him through their unity. Jesus prayed passionately for His church to come into its full authority on the earth because they would be one just as He is one. Paul taught that The Church is called of God to lead a broken world to know Christ through the Unity of the Spirit and the Unity of the Faith! So we must be repentant and responsive to God's divine imperative. He basically guaranteed the Father that we will obey Him. O, how I pray we will not disappoint Him.

---

[24] Revelation 12:11 NLT

"I have revealed You to the ones You gave Me . . . and they have kept Your word. Now they know that everything I have is a gift from You, for I have passed on to them the message You gave Me. They accepted it . . . My prayer is not for the world, but for those (church) You gave Me . . . they are staying here . . . I am departing. Holy Father, You have given Me Your name, now protect them by the power of Your name so that they (church) will be united just as we are."

John 17:6–11 NLT

CHAPTER TWO

ONENESS UNITY

"My Prayer is not for the world, but for those you have given me, because they belong to you. Now I am departing from the world; they are staying in this world, but I am coming to you. Holy Father, you have given me your name, now protect them by the power of your name so that they will be united just as we are. I pray that they will all be one, just as you and I are one- as you are in me, Father, and I am in you. And may they be in us so that the world will believe you sent me. I have given them the glory you gave me, so they may be one as we are one. I am in them and you are in me. May they experience such perfect unity that you love them as much as you love me."
John 17:9, 11, 21–23 NLT

We were created to live in the same harmonious unity as the Godhead. ". . . let us make man in our image, to be like us . . . so . . . he created them male and female . . . he breathed the breath of (His) life into the man . . . this explains why . . . a man is joined to his wife and the two are united into one."[25] "I appeal to you . . . to live in harmony with each other. Let there be no divisions in the church. Rather be of one mind, united in thought and purpose."[26] The highest testimony of the power and presence of God on the earth is the oneness and unity of the Godhead demonstrated daily through the body of Christ. For such a multi-diversified nuclear family or church family to each sacrifice and willingly yield their own independence, to become the living expression of the interdependent, loving Godhead, is a phenomenon so compelling as to be almost impossible to ignore. The world will not be able to ignore the dynamics of our Holy God rising out of the heart of that kind of united reality. Even more awesome to contemplate is a community-wide—yes, even an ultimate world-wide—impact of the glorious gospel of Jesus through a unified Church only known and recognized in the community and the world simply as "The Church"! It is different from anything like it in the whole world. It is a stunning and supernatural statement that defies being disregarded.

A family in our community experienced the reality and the power of the local church community working together in corporate unity. Together, we engaged the city manager, city

---

[25] Genesis 1:26–27; 2:7, 24 NLT
[26] 1 Corinthians 1:10–11 NLT

ONENESS UNITY

council, local businesses, and local church members to build a three-bedroom home in six days for a needy family. Before, during, and after the build, the stunning news in the community was, "The Church is doing this? Wow, I think I'm going back to church." The fact we did this in love together, without interchurch or pastoral self-seeking, was clearly recognized as we all laid down our reputations for Jesus and one another. The shocking impact on the whole community has strengthened our desire for increased unity among the churches.

.This not only declares there is a God in the world to be reckoned with, but the overwhelming impact, and influence of the footprint of righteousness and truth is the paramount reality in the world and requires a deliberate personal decision.

Does that sound delusional to you? You say it could never happen. It's just pie in the sky and not realistic! Was Jesus just dreaming the impossible dream, or delusional, when He said, The Church will ". . . all be perfected into one. Then the world will know . . ."[27] Think for a moment. We have trouble with oneness and unity because we think so singularly, and, at best, locally. God thinks globally about everything. Therefore, God made us in His image to express Him in oneness! He did not create us to be millions of singular, separated, scattered, and disconnected units responsible to unrelatedly bring the world to Christ. Everything He has done and is doing is accomplished in unity.

---

[27] John 17:23 NLT

For example, all created things are made "after its kind" in families and in churches. The apostle Paul taught about things being accomplished in the kingdom of God, "together" with "one another." Corporate prayer is the one most powerful and effective unified and unifying work of the church. "My house shall be called a house of prayer."[28] Therefore, I believe we have viewed oneness and unity as an option, sort of an extra credit project if we have time or want to make a good impression. As a result, we have ignored God's concept of worldwide evangelism, and created our own ideas for "personal evangelism." They have been useful tools in reaching many people for Jesus's sake. However, I believe we have missed the joy and pleasure of learning the hard lessons of coming together in the genuine life-style of unity. Presenting such a oneness shocks the unbelieving world around us when they see and experience the reality of God's love in the unified voice and attitude of the Christians in their community. The impact upon them influences their thinking and opens their minds to receive the impartation of truth. You see, it's not delusional. It is, in fact, a reality The Church is unwilling to pay the price of self-sacrifice to experience it.

It was not a fluke of circumstances the disciples heard the deep passion of Jesus's heart as He prayed for His Church. They experienced, first hand, the incredible oneness of the Godhead. They heard the priority Jesus put on prayer as He expressed His passion for the unity of The Church. It was

---

[28] Luke 19:46 NAS

ONENESS UNITY

deeply set in their hearts: prayer and unity! They weren't aware that in a few days they would hear those divinely established priorities again when the Holy Spirit would come and The Church would be born.[29] They were ready for the challenge to lead. For three years He had discipled them. Unknown to them, they were being prepared to yield to Him, to live His life in them.[30] Little did they know they would draw on His discipleship training often in the years to come. The timing of this prayer was set before the foundation of the world. Those final days included His crash course on life and leadership essentials: servanthood, a submissive spirit, a heart after God, a teachable spirit, a passion for His church, and laying down their lives as their permanent way of life until the day of their natural death.[31]

Therefore, this was no flunky angel prayer. Nor was it the powerful prayer of the mighty archangel Gabriel. Oh, no! This prayer ministry required none other than the great High Priest, Jesus Christ, the Son of the Living God! It must not be heard as a suggestion or as an option! This prayer necessitated the holy imprint of the High Priest for it to be heard and received as nothing less than His divine imperative! The Trinity, the Godhead Himself, the ultimate expression of Unity, was passionately declaring His desire " . . . that they will all be one, *just as you and I are one* . . . so that the world will believe You sent Me." He set the standard for

---

[29] Acts 2:42–47 NLT
[30] Colossians 1:26–29 NLT
[31] John 13—21; 1 John 3:16 NLT

unity in The Church: no compromises, no concessions, no cultural adjustments, and no mediocre, half-hearted lifestyle. Can you even imagine competition, comparison, divisions, and disputes going on in the Godhead?

Competing for greater recognition, and concerned about doctrinal positions, especially those related to the Holy Spirit? Just allow your own mind to imagine that possibility. It is silly isn't it? Please, let your mind compare your own thoughts and attitudes about fellow believers and churches, with the simplicity and purity of the phrase, *"just as we are one . . ."*! Are you finding yourself concerned about what that may require of you? Or, are you challenged to discover the pleasures and the pain in the journey to Oneness with Jesus and His people, especially the ones who believe doctrines you don't agree with? Or believers of different races? Are you resisting the feeling you now have to think about this? The truth is, to be a Kingdom Christian, you have to exercise your choice. When you choose Him and His ways, it requires thinking and changing continually. Jesus is not an "add-on" God; added on to the rest of your responsibilities! He "is *the* way, *the* truth, *the* life . . ."[32] Actually, Jesus makes it very clear; ". . . You must love the Lord your God with all your heart, all your soul, and all your mind . . ."[33] Let me say it another way. Being a follower of Jesus Christ is your vocation. Your avocation is your career. You are not a nurse who happens to be a Christian. You are a Christian who happens to

---

[32] John 14:6 NLT
[33] Matthew 22:37 NLT

ONENESS UNITY

be a nurse. Therefore, when Jesus prayed that we Christians would become one just as the Godhead is one, He was not suggesting we modify it until we like it. The standard is set, so ". . . choose you this day whom you will serve.[34]

The unity He speaks of is more than mere unanimity. It is so much more than an acceptable attitude of "getting along" with fellow Christians. This unity rests upon the unity of the Holy Spirit and His life in us. It is not a mind-to-mind concept; it is spirit to spirit! His Spirit in you, and in me becomes the holy force of God that draws us into an undeniable longing to be united into one dynamic expression of the love of Christ. In other words, oneness empowers us to be and do together what we could never accomplish as lone rangers.

> The Church has been willing to substitute good-enough-for-now unity. Community unity events and projects are recognized as the ultimate expression of the unity of the body of Christ. Although they are a powerful testimony of Jesus's love, they also demonstrate how divided and disconnected The Church really is. Unfortunately, the sin of self still rules The Church because oneness is not a priority. The real issue is the "me-first" syndrome; my church, my programs, my ministry, my schedule, my reputation, and

---

[34] Joshua 24:15 NLT

my circle of friends and church relationships. Self rules The Church. The faithful sheep follow their shepherd into their own separate sphere of influence, for their own reputation in the community. Their desire is to stand above the other churches rather than stand with them. It's the comparison and competition game again; the good, better and the best grading system. What a tragedy!

The unity Jesus longs for is so much more than a meager remnant gathering of Christians all together in one room, name tags in place, and calling it unity. No, Jesus is praying for a permanent lifestyle of kingdom life unity. A unity where the Christians of the local Bible-believing churches, individually and corporately, care more about Jesus and His message impacting the whole community together than "me and my church." It is a unity that lives in an obvious corporate, cross-cultural, and cross-denominational love for one another. It is the unified expression of Jesus Christ that causes the unbelieving world around us to be drawn irresistibly to become followers of Jesus.

Of course, this means God will put us through His baptisms of fire to keep us pure in the maturing process of unity. His fiery trials reveal to us what He sees of self remaining in us. The recognition of it causes us to gladly embrace His way and yield to the process He uses to shape us more into His image. The more we embrace the purifying process, the greater the empowering grace of God is released from Him, and through Him into the church and the world. Centuries ago—100 A.D. to 310 A.D.—more than a million martyred Christians became the seed God planted to raise up His anticipated Bride-Church "for such a time as this."[35] Just as those martyred saints lay down their lives to maintain and sustain the unity of a very verbal, and obviously visible Church, it is still the passionate heart cry of Jesus that we do the same. We can no longer "get by" ignoring our Bridegroom's desire. We are responsible to Him, and to His Bride, to grow "to be mature . . . to the full and complete standard of Christ."[36] His unity and maturity will follow the brokenness of our self ways, because the life of the Spirit means death to our self-driven flesh.

When my wife and I married, we were so immature. In not-so-subtle ways, we made one another aware of the "right way" to do those really important things such as how the toilet paper should roll, how to do the dishes, or how to squeeze the toothpaste, how to repair an item, ad nauseum. Unity was nowhere to be seen. However, our covenant to love one another regardless, along with our experience of walking in that covenant, and our age, taught us that maturity dismisses the small stuff. We learned the only things worth disrupting our lives over were those things that will make a difference in eternity. My wife coined the phrase, "in terms of eternity, what does it matter?" That eliminates a lot of stuff the devil would like to use to distract us from our commitment to Jesus

---

[35] Esther 4:14 NLT
[36] Ephesians 4:13 NLT

and one another. That lifestyle of oneness has had the unintended results of influencing and impacting many other marriages. Our visible oneness has had a powerful influence that changes lives. The Church must choose to live in a lifestyle of verbal and visible oneness. It requires active and determined commitment to Jesus and one another. Only lifestyle oneness will cause ". . . the world to know . . . that God loves them *as much as* He loves Jesus."[37]

---

[37] John 17:23 NLT

CHAPTER THREE

SPIRIT UNITY

"Always be humble and gentle. Be patient with each other, making allowance for each other's faults because of your love. Make every effort to keep yourselves united in the Spirit, binding yourselves together with peace. For there is one body and one Spirit, just as you have been called to one glorious hope for the future. There is one Lord, one faith, one baptism, and One God and Father, who is over all and in all and living through all.
Ephesians 4:2–6 NLT

*T*he language in this passage calls for determination to take deliberate action to diligently preserve the unity of the Spirit. Therefore, because unity is our possession through being born again, it is necessary for every believer to take personal responsibility to guard that unity against injury and loss. We are commanded to personally protect and preserve the unity of the Spirit with our lives, in the bond of peace.[38] Some of the issues that require our diligence to guard against in our own lives and in fellow believers lives are divisions, quarrels, jealousy, rivalry, selfish ambition, impure motives, disharmony, slander, factions, and idolatry.[39] The imperative for the unity of the Spirit is that, individually and corporately, we are totally committed to loving one another in the body of Christ.

Love is the foundation for the unity of the Spirit, and peace is the evidence that love is alive and active. "Above all, clothe yourselves with love, which binds us all together in perfect unity. And let the peace that comes from Christ rule in your hearts . . ."[40] Therefore, the peace of Christ that lives in us through the indwelling presence of the Holy Spirit is the bond wrapped around The Church, holding Christians together in unity. When peace is crumbling, it is because our unity has been disturbed by our fading love for Jesus Christ. It is, therefore, necessary that "we keep choosing to be . . . humble and gentle . . . patient with each other's faults because

---

[38] Ephesians 4:13; Romans 12:18 NLT
[39] 1 Corinthians 1:10–12; Philippians 1:15–17; Galatians 5:19–21 NLT
[40] Colossians 3:12–15; Ephesians 4:2–3 NLT

SPIRIT UNITY

of our love. Make every effort to keep yourselves together with peace." The motivation is our consistent prayer and sensitivity to the promptings of the Holy Spirit concerning one another. This is our responsibility. The Holy Spirit assigned us to diligence in making every effort to maintain the unity of the Spirit. Unity requires an equal partnership in fulfilling God's purposes, just like the equal partnership of the Godhead. We have either been irresponsible in keeping the unity, or we have believed God will do something about the unity of the believers Himself. I suspect we would prefer God will one day do a supernatural worldwide fly-over, scattering unity dust on the saints. Then He is responsible for unity in The Church. However, the language Paul uses here is commanding and challenging. We cannot avoid this mandate. The fact that The Church is generally weak and ineffective is evidence enough of our self-centered arrogance and disobedience. Like Cain, if we are not our brother's keeper, we will surely become our brother's killer! Unity is intentional. It is your responsibility! It is the personal privilege and responsibility of every believer. The big picture idea here is that it conveys the idea of personal exertion. It literally means we believers have the privilege to make unity in the Spirit our business by watching, praying, maintaining, encouraging, challenging, and loving, bringing into everyone's life, ". . . the peace the world cannot give.[41] Our unity is established within us at our new birth—His divine nature born in us by the Holy Spirit. We are spiritually bound together by the same

---

[41] John 14:27 NLT

Holy Spirit. Therefore, we are challenged to be personally responsible to stand guard and work at not allowing anything to injure or ruin the unity in or of the Holy Spirit! Step into the fray and pray, and call the saints to accountability. No divisions; stop talking and taking sides. Stand in Christ and call fellow Jesus followers to obedience to the living word of God.

Furthermore, this unity in the Spirit is not merely a request to try your hardest to get involved to the best of our ability. That would deny the mandate, making it semi-optional. No! It is the call to the privilege of yielding our spirit-driven inner man, to remain unwilling to accept anything in the body of Christ, other than the peace of God. His established love within us becomes our living motivation to be *one* in Him that results in His glorious peace. The completion of this whole picture is that the unity in the Spirit, is fully expressed when we intentionally live and move and exist[42] together in *one*: "One body, one Spirit, one hope, . . . one Lord, One Faith, one Baptism, and one God and Father, Who is over all and in all and living through all."[43]

This is why unity is the responsibility of The Church. Jesus's prayer requires that we must ". . . work out our own salvation . . ."[44] We must repent. We must lay down our flesh. We must ask forgiveness, give forgiveness, pray often and much, make personal sacrifices, love much, and give our

---

[42] Acts 17:28 NLT
[43] Ephesians 4:4–6 NLT
[44] Philippians 2:12–13 NAS

lives away for the glory of His Kingdom. Unity is about the big picture—The Church. It's about corporate unity of all of Jesus's followers and His Word, from the local community to the whole world. God never intends anything He does to be only local. Everything He creates, desires, and releases is about Him and His glory through His Church world-wide!For example, when the pastors and churches of your community agree to come together with their diverse but unified people for a corporate expression of Jesus, it releases the powerful presence of God upon the community. This is way more than mere community spirit or community cooperation. Any civic group can do that. But this? This is unity of another kingdom and kind. This is Godhead unity! It is a worldwide kind of unity that will have the same impact of the Holy Spirit anywhere it is expressed in the world. Wherever a corporate impact of the presence of God is released, it leaves behind a level of receptivity of God and His ways that deeply impacts the hearts and hopes of those who gave it away and those who received it. Another wonderful side-effect of corporate impact is that not one of those who minister, or those who receive the ministry, seems to notice or even care about the names of the churches. It always is about the Spirit of peace, bound together with the corporate expression of love that draws people to Jesus. It's not about the people being identified by their name and church. It is about Jesus! I pray often that The Church will have an ever increasing abundance of encounters with the Holy Spirit just like that. I get so delighted telling stories about these encounters in the context

GOD'S PASSIONATE DESIRE... for unity in the church!

of this kind of self-sacrificing cooperation. However, invariably my excitement is challenged because it appears to some of my fellow believers I have been too verbal about the power and presence of the Holy Spirit. That, I discovered, causes some caution about further corporate unity relationships. By the way, from God's perspective, unity is not about temporary corporate community projects. It is, rather, a lifestyle of being together in the context of Christian fellowship that ultimately generates ongoing Christian relationships. Those ongoing Christian relationships mature in deepening love that establishes a unity held together by the love and peace we enjoy in that relationship. It is this dynamic that causes unity to be such a powerful tool for drawing people to Jesus. I am theologically and experientially a charismatic Christian. However, I do not have any hesitation about relating to a fellow believer for the sake of kingdom influence and impact. Jesus, His glorious gospel, and His incomparable ways, mean more to me than doctrinal question marks about someone's life. The scripture exhorts us to follow Jesus and "lay down [our] life for the sheep . . ."[45] It is vital that we learn to love beyond these roadblocks and preserve the unity of the Spirit from injury or loss. Love is still God's criteria for maturity. The measure of our love for one another demonstrates our level of maturity. I am aware we Jesus followers have given one another sufficient opportunity to wonder more than a little bit about each other's love. "However, most important of all, . . . show deep love for each other, for love covers a

---

[45] John 10:11, 15 NLT

multitude of sins."[46] May I encourage us to let love rule our hearts and our mouths as we corporately minister together. Some Christians are embarrassingly indiscreet when talking about Jesus. Social manners are sometimes cast off as though they are hindering shackles, where others may be offensive for other reasons. Wisdom and love will recognize the power of laying down our own flesh reasons that will release His persuasive truth into the hearts of seeking people.

There are so many illustrations of egregious, and sinful behavior that hinder the unity in the Holy Spirit. You have heard and seen them as the flesh resists the glory of His Presence in the midst of the persuasive ministry of the Holy Spirit. However, your experience in the local church tells you the apostle Paul clearly understood the sinful conflicts behind the walls of the church. "I appeal to you . . . by the authority of our Lord Jesus Christ, to live in harmony with each other. Let there be no divisions in the church . . I have been told of your quarrel . . . has Christ been divided into factions? . . . and you compare yourselves with each other using yourselves as the standard . . ."[47] What do we have here? Immature Christian sibling rivalry in the church. Demonstrated daily across the world, church leaders and their followers, compare themselves like insecure adolescents with their competitors. They carefully observe one another's churches, comparing themselves with the others in the interest of competing more successfully. Truthfully, this is as sickening to write about as

---
[46] I Peter 4:8 NLT
[47] I Corinthians 1:10–13 NLT

it is to observe. It is spiritually impossible to love one another and minister together in unity when the peace and love of God are merely a doctrine! This is living hypocrisy, mere pretense. Deep in our hearts we are consumed with the knowledge that the church across town has greater numbers, reputation, and finances, and it appears their arrogance is proof.

For my heart, here is the most painful part. The Church of Jesus, His Bride, has embraced as a godly and biblical model, the production of domesticated and further acculturated christianettes, who have not been discipled! We appear to be more concerned about how we are marketing our brand than we are about taking the time necessary to make disciples. There are churches that have wonderful and good people who want to know and walk with God, but have only had, what I call, a conviction experience. They have not experienced a genuine conversion to the truth and the way of Jesus because they were not taught how to appropriate His life as a new follower of Him. They have been domesticated and acculturated but not discipled! "You will always harvest what you plant. Those who live only to satisfy their own sinful nature will harvest decay and death from that sinful nature. However, those who live to please the Spirit will harvest everlasting life from the Spirit."[48]

The holy injunction to ". . .make every effort to keep yourselves united in the Spirit . . ."[49] is God's gracious desire to enjoy this unity in the Holy Spirit, with individual believers

---

[48] Galatians 6:8 NLT
[49] Ephesians 4:3 NL

in the same growing relationship, as He desires with all believers. Therefore, every believer is called to lay down their life to diligently preserve the unity of The Church through the power and presence of the Holy Spirit.

CHAPTER FOUR

FAITH UNITY

"Now these are the gifts Christ gave to the church: the apostles, the prophets, the evangelists, and the pastors and teachers. Their responsibility is to equip God's people to do his work and build up the church, the body of Christ. This will continue until we all come to such unity in our faith and knowledge of God's Son that we will be mature in the Lord, measuring up to the full and complete standard of Christ."
Ephesians 4:11–13 NLT

God says He has only one Church. Actually, we are told in the Word it is imperative that The Church must be the living testimony of that fact. The unity of heaven must be displayed ". . . on earth as it is in heaven."[50] This one-church unity is not just a hypothetical possibility; it is expected because it is attainable! Unity is the unfinished business of The Church. We need some people like Joshua and Caleb. The people of Israel resisted their challenge, saying they couldn't finish the task of entering the Promised Land because the obstacles were too many and difficult. However, forty years later, they came back and the two old warriors united their minds and hearts again upon the promise of God, moved out in faith, and took possession of their promise. They believed God when no one else would join them. Their unwavering faith in God strengthened them to not bow to satan's distractions.

The real question here is do we really believe God is serious about the unity of The Church? "If you love Me obey My commandments."[51] Let's be honest. If we believe God has mandated that The Church become *one* as the Godhead is *one*, that The Church make every effort to maintain the unity of the Spirit upon which He founded The Church, that The Church involve itself in discipling the saints to the level of maturity in Jesus Christ that compels them to live together with other saints in the unity of the Faith,[52] then why haven't

---

[50] Matthew 6:10; Ephesians 4:13 NLT
[51] John 14:25 NLT
[52] John 17:23; Ephesians 4:2–3, 11–13 NLT

FAITH UNITY

we accomplished it yet? My personal belief is that we have chosen to address this matter from one of the following viewpoints: it's not that important . . . yet, it's optional, it's God's responsibility as an end-times project, or it means sacrificing my flesh and its glory, for His mandate to love the world so much I will ". . . sacrifice my life for the sheep . . ."[53]

It is really difficult to be neutral about this. At the root of all disunity and division is the flesh. This is the point of the struggle between our flesh and our spirit. When our mind is set on knowing Him,[54] we have very little struggle winning over our flesh-man, our human nature. However, life is filled with distractions, many of which are good things. However, when those really "good things" that distract us from pressing on to know Him, become "main things," they become idols to us. Truthfully, they are the result of our own "evil desires."[55] Here is the picture: we know God wants unity in the body of Christ, and we intend to disciple one another to the necessary maturity in Jesus that compels us to be a part of making unity happen. However, "the spirit is willing but the flesh is weak!"[56] Ultimately, we cave in to the lesser things distracting us, while we wait for a more convenient time to obey God. A key question at the decision point is, whose kingdom am I really building? His or mine? Will I put my flesh's agenda before the revealed agenda of God, or do I obey the agenda of God and "For His sake discard everything else, counting

---

[53] John 10:15 NLT
[54] Philippians 3:10 AMP
[55] James 1:14–15 NLT
[56] Matthew 26:41 NLT

it all as garbage, so that I will gain Christ and become one with Him"?[57] Only you can win this struggle. The only way to lose a fight is to stop fighting. Like Joshua and Caleb, stay in the struggle. Jesus said, ". . . if any of you wants to be My follower, you must turn from your selfish ways, take up your cross daily, and follow Me."[58]

Another side of this flesh versus Spirit battle is with the mandate for the unity of the faith. That is because we seem to believe we may have to "give up" a belief, value, or doctrine we will not compromise. O people of God, the unity of the faith spoken of here simply requires us to share together in the same gospel message by which all believers are born again! What makes us *"one just as we are one"*[59] is we are engaged to the same groom—Jesus Christ, the Son of the Living God, by faith alone. It is our flesh that searches the scriptural landscape for noneternal life issues, about which we then justify our unwillingness to invest in the unity of the faith. I am quite certain, for example, some have already launched their flesh upon the apostles, prophets, evangelists, pastors, and teachers doctrine. Let me stop to say this: at the heart of every problem is the problem in your heart. I assure you, there are a minimum of three factions disagreeing about these five gifts; the Mainline church, the Charismatic church, and the Evangelical church. I have two questions. Will anyone be born of the Spirit because we settled this issue? Will any new or growing

---

[57] Philippians 3:8–9 NLT
[58] Luke 9:23 NLT
[59] John 17:21–23 NLT

believer receive better or worse discipling because we settle this issue? Please understand what is at stake here. It's not about the title someone possesses or whether that title is permanent or temporary. The issue here is that people are fully trained and discipled in the Word and ways of God, who will in turn do the same with others. Thus, we are building up the body of Christ. Each one will grow in the knowledge of the Son of God, not book knowledge, but heart knowledge, discipled into each life. The more each one grows in intimacy with Jesus, the more their maturity guides them into ever increasing unity with the saints of God, whoever they were taught by, and wherever they have come from.

I believe this may be why we are so skittish about the unity of the Faith. Our differences and divisions are over issues of function and fellowship, and methods of learning and growing in the truth. These are simply matters of personal preference. All we have left to divide over is how we preach and teach the Word of God. A simple phrase for unity is "the same as," which is just what God wants. He has one church, His church, "… one body, one spirit, one hope, one Lord, one faith, one baptism, and one God and Father Who is over all, and in all, and living through all."[60] The choice, then, is to recognize those who are born of the Spirit as the same as all the others who are born of the Spirit.

The wonderful truth, if we will embrace it, is that the gospel makes us one and the same. Though our flesh-man demands public recognition of our particular purity of

---

[60] Ephesians 4:4–6 NLT

doctrine and distinctive methods in the presentation of that gospel, we are nonetheless the same. I grew up in a denomination that taught me very well about the four doctrines that were our "distinctives." These, we thought, would set us apart, possibly even a cut above every other evangelical, Bible-believing group. As I grew in the Lord and His Word, and discussed the truth of that Word with fellow Pastors and Christians, I discovered they had the same doctrines, but by different titles. My first confused thoughts were about finding out how many other denominations were just like us. Are we really all supposed to be that much alike? Maturity in the Word and experience helped to sort all these doctrines out for me. In the next chapter, I will share how God clarified them to my satisfaction. In the meantime, let's take a quick look back at where we have been in this journey toward living in, and being the living demonstration of the unity in The Church.

Jesus's prayer in John 17 beautifully illustrates the "one-and-the-same" model for the unity of the Faith. "I pray that they will all be one, just as You and I are one—as You are in Me . . . and I am in You . . ." Therefore, the kind of unity Jesus prayed for is a one and the same—"just as We are one . . ." This unity is transferable; "as You are in Me, and I am in You . . ." When you and I were born again of the Holy Spirit,[61] He came to live in our spirit. Upon His desire to make me into His image from the inside-out, the divine exchange was made. His divine nature took over mine, and mine became

---

[61] John 3:5–8 NLT

His.[62] Unity—being "one and the same"—is accomplished in the Holy Spirit by the Holy Spirit. Now Paul strongly instructs that we are now responsible to maintain that unity with the Godhead, and with all those who have also come into that same unity with Him. That is the unity of the Spirit. Unity is the result of love! Jesus came to earth to find His Bride. He is finding her through the ministry of His Holy Spirit in the lives of His people who are His Church. Jesus's passionate desire is that His one Church will fulfill this passion through the incredible miracle of being willing to die to our flesh and embrace the unity of the Faith.

We have all come into His marvelous spiritual kingdom by faith in Christ alone. Not one of us has come with more than anyone else, nor has anyone received more salvation than all the rest of us. Because of who we are, and Who He is becoming in our daily lives, each one will grow and mature in Him in differing patterns of development. However, the basis of our unity is our salvation. His love draws us to the faith. Our love draws us into unity with His Church. That love and unity brings to The Church the peace that passes all understanding. This is why we are willing to take the responsibility given to us to ". . . make every effort to keep ourselves united in the Spirit."[63] It is our intention to preserve this unity of the Spirit and Faith from any damage to its life, integrity, and credibility in our part of the world. Therefore, we sustain this unity through praying for and caring for one another. In

---

[62] 2 Peter 1:3–4 NLT
[63] Ephesians 4:3 NLT

addition, we willingly provide ample testimony of our unity through deliberate and cooperative engagement in verbal and visible demonstrations of that fact. The practicality of our responsibility in preserving our unity from injury or loss, lies in our willingness to daily make conscious decisions to deny our flesh to have its own way, while choosing to deliberately yield to the control of the Holy Spirit: ". . . I want Your will to be done, not mine."[64]

Of course, this is a unity that reaches beyond the sentimental Christian unity events that are often laced with unity lingo and somewhat pompous pretense. I think we will observe an example of that real kind of unity in the next chapter.

---

[64] Matthew 26:39 NLT

CHAPTER FIVE

UNITY MODEL
THE MOST IMPORTANT THING!

"Let me now remind you, dear brothers and sisters, of the Good News I preached to you before. You welcomed it then, and you still stand firm in it. It is this Good News that saves you if you continue to believe the message I told you—unless, of course, you believed something that was never true in the first place. I passed on to you what was most important and what had also been passed on to me, Christ died for our sins, just as the Scriptures said. He was buried, and he was raised from the dead on the third day, just as the Scriptures said."
1 Corinthians 15:1–4 NLT

> As for me, God forbid that I should boast about anything except the cross of our Lord Jesus Christ. Because of that cross, my interest in this world died long ago, and the world's interest in me is also long dead. It doesn't make any difference now whether we have been circumcised or not. What counts is whether we really have been changed into new and different people.
> Galatians 6:14–15 NLT

*F*or years I prayed for increased revelation about a practical plan for a model of unity that could be implemented in my life, my home, the church I pastored, and the community in which I served the Lord. I was asking for a simple transferable model.

One day, almost twenty years ago, I read an article in a newsletter published by a highly regarded pastor/author. It was written by his pastor friend. These two faithful men had prayed for years that the unity of The Church would become a reality in their city. The example of their personal love and unity has resulted in great glory to God and His kingdom in their city and across the country. Perhaps it is profitable to mention that one was a Charismatic and the other a Baptist. True to the humble spirit I had touched in reading the article, there was the statement of permission for use in creating a burning passion for love and unity in The Church. I have used this model in my own life, family, church, and community since that day. I have chosen to use his outline as the

THE MOST IMPORTANT THING!

framework for this chapter.

"In all matters of life and godliness"[65] ". . . the most important thing"[66] is Christ and Him crucified! Quite often, we are distracted from Him by our own fleshly efforts to build our church. The rules, doctrines, and interpretations we establish are meant to keep us focused on Him and His ways. However, the purity of this focus is challenged when we think the order of doctrinal importance needs to be changed. Therefore, for the sake of the preferred doctrinal order of our church or denomination, we move a certain doctrine to a lower level than it really deserves. In so doing, we may compromise the unity of The Church, and endanger its nature. By treating important doctrines as though they are merely matters of personal preference, we sin against Jesus Christ who bought us with His blood. .

On the other hand, we may also change the order of importance by moving a doctrine to a higher level than it deserves. That, too, may fracture and divide the body of Christ. A church sign near where I live, boldly declares, "Preaching the true gospel from the only true Bible, the original KJV!" Now, here are some well-meaning Christians, choosing to make a Bible version the test of real faith. Because you believe, The Church will, or will not, go through the tribulation, or because you do, or don't speak in tongues, or believe in the baptism of the Spirit, or baptize infants, I should not make it my privilege or responsibility to question your commitment

---

[65] 2 Peter 1:3 NAS
[66] 1 Corinthians 15:3 NLT

GOD'S PASSIONATE DESIRE... for unity in the church!

to Christ. I should not treat those issues as if they should be of greater importance than they are. "It doesn't matter whether we have been circumcised or not. What counts is whether we have been transformed into a new creation."[67] When I do treat those issues irresponsibly, I offend the blood of Christ that was shed to redeem one church.

There also are some issues I should keep to myself, and give you the same freedom. There are other matters that should have a picket fence around them. After all, the Christian neighborhood should offer an atmosphere where deep friendships will be developed, even if we do attend different churches. However, there are some issues around which you and I must build a brick wall. Martin Luther said, "Here I stand, I can do no other." Yes, there are doctrines worth fighting for. It is extremely important, for the sake of the unity of The Church, to discover which truths fit into that category.

The Church must be a powerful, living example of truth and unity. First, we must maintain biblical truth as the standard of righteousness and truth for all men, in all places, for all time. Second, we must maintain biblical freedom as the standard of love and acceptance among those who stand uncompromisingly for biblical truth.

I am proposing here a model consisting of four levels of doctrine that may help us reach the goal of the unity of the faith. At least it may help us sort out our flesh-centered thinking concerning Jesus's ultimate intention to possess a

---

[67] Galatians 6:14–15 NLT

pure, holy, and unified Bride-Church.

LEVEL ONE—Brick Wall Doctrine

These doctrines form the foundation of The Church. What makes them so important is they are what I refer to as Eternal Life doctrines. They are the foundational doctrines for establishing the unity of the faith. Of these we confidently say, "No Compromise"! For these, we stand and fight, when necessary. The divisions these doctrines create, we eagerly welcome.[68] These truths will divide fellow believers from those who are "wolves in sheep's clothing."[69] This speaks to the exclusivity of the gospel of redemption. Yes, there is only one way to heaven. "I am the Way, the Truth, the Life, no one comes to My Father, but by Me."[70] We either lead people to Him, or they choose their own destiny in hell. Of necessity, it will create a holy war of righteousness and truth being challenged and opposed by a culture that believes it must resist a holy God Who longs to bring them the very freedom they are so desperately seeking.

There are two truth views. Each is at the root of how we choose to live our lives. One truth view is defined by God. The other is defined by the individual. First, we have the God view that believes truth is objective, absolute, and universal. This is because truth exists outside of us. It is, therefore, constant and eternal. It is the standard of right and wrong. It

---

[68] Hebrews 4:12–13 NAS
[69] Matthew 7:15 NAS
[70] John 14:6 NAS

applies to all people, in all places, for all time. Truth is established by God. The second view of truth is the "me" view of truth. It's all about "me." It is subjective. Truth is determined by my circumstances and feelings today. Truth is situational, relative, and continually changing, depending on how I feel and what I feel, who I am with, where I am, and when something good or bad happens. Truth is determined by me!

We must stand uncompromisingly committed to God's truth. We will not be moved. Without embarrassment and with covenant love, we will fight the good fight of faith.[71]

This is Brick Wall Doctrine
These are *eternal life issues.*
The Virgin Birth of Jesus Christ
The Death and Resurrection of Jesus Christ
The Efficacy of the Blood of Jesus Christ
The inerrancy and authority of the Scriptures
The Sovereignty of God
The Godhead — Father, Son and Holy Spirit
The Second Coming of Jesus Christ
The Judgment
Salvation by grace through Faith alone

At stake here is the integrity and credibility of The Church! For these we will die! These are Eternal Life doctrines, the fundamental foundation of our lives in Christ Jesus. These

---

[71] 1 Timothy 1:18 NAS

are the most important things.[72] These are what define The Church—the body of Christ! Upon these we form the unity of the faith. Nothing else! Nothing less! For these we will stand. We cannot and we will not compromise! Defending these Eternal Life doctrines together in the unity of the Holy Spirit and the unity of the faith, will clarify and strengthen our one voice and its impact on the unsaved world around us.

LEVEL TWO—Picket Fence Doctrine

These are matters of *fellowship and function* in your local church! In these, we are flexible, accepting, and understanding. Above all, we think and act in love, and are not thinking, speaking, or acting in a condescending or condemning manner toward others that do not think as we do. As we learn, share, and relate to one another, we set boundaries. These are not lines of division and separation. Nor does it imply they are not important matters. They are essential and necessary in your church. However, they should never become points of division in the body of Christ. They are extremely valuable within the ministry and circle of Fellowship and Function of your church. Inside the Brick Wall, the worldwide community of Christians, is a neighborhood with Picket Fences that identify their particular houses. But notice, they are Picket Fences. We can see through and over them. There are gates with handles on both sides that invite us to come over to share the good things of God together. These are not walls of separation. They are acceptable boundaries, but they

---

[72] 1 Corinthians 15:3 NAS

are not for thinking of ourselves more highly than we ought.[73] They are not statements of spiritual pride and arrogance or pronouncements of our special uniqueness in the Christian neighborhood. Oh no, they are simply doctrines of fellowship and function for the increased fulfillment of your experience in Jesus Christ through your church.

This is Picket Fence Doctrine

The wise and discerning Christian will discover more of these doctrines as their journey in Jesus matures.

- Water Baptism—Immersion or Pouring
- Infant Baptism / Infant Dedication
- Forms of church government
- Baptism in the Holy Spirit
- Gifts of the Spirit
- Five-fold Ministry Gifts (Apostle, Prophet, Evangelist, Pastor, Teacher)
- The Lord's Supper / Communion—(style and frequency)
- Calvinism
- Arminianism
- Worship Style
- Women in Ministry
- Divorce and Remarriage

These are not Eternal Life issues, but they do add to the meaning and fulfillment of your Eternal Life through Jesus

---

[73] Romans 12:3 NAS

Christ. Therefore, we are charged by God to "make every effort to preserve (guard from loss or injury) the unity of the Spirit."[74] For the sake of the unity of the body of Christ, do all in your ability to maintain the influence and authenticity of the life and message of your church in your city. These matters are indeed vital to the effectiveness of the Fellowship and Function of your circle of relationships, but they will never be worth the pain and agony caused by drawing lines of division. In fact, our love and desire to maintain and sustain the unity of the Spirit and of the faith as fellow believers strengthen The Church and the message of the cross in these end time days.

LEVEL THREE—Backyard Doctrine

These are matters of *learning and growing* in the Lord and relationship with fellow Christians. They are necessary to the life and love of the body of Christ as it is exemplified in and through your church. Of course, they must never become points of division of separation among fellow believers. When someone's doctrine affects the reality or outcome of their eternal salvation, then we must erect our Brick Wall. If it affects the Fellowship and Function of your church, then put up a Picket Fence. However, if it affects neither, then sit right down in your lounge chair and share with your Christian neighbors your recent discoveries in the Word. As you do, you will both become more fitly joined together[75] in the body of Christ.

---

[74] Ephesians 4:3 NAS
[75] Ephesians 4:16 NAS

GOD'S PASSIONATE DESIRE... for unity in the church!

This is Backyard Doctrine
Discipleship Methods
Eschatology and Bible Prophecy
Bible Translations
Bible Reading Patterns
Usage of Alcohol / Tobacco
Personal Devotional life and Prayer
Altar Calls
Christian Entertainment and Trends
Government and Politics

All of these are vital to your personal growth as a Christian. However, be assured that none of these are matters for quarrels or separations. Relax and enjoy your fellow Christian. You may even have some meaningful conversation about these issues, but be assured, they love Jesus just as you do. "You owe no man anything except the debt of love."[76]

LEVEL FOUR — CLOSET DOCTRINE

These are matters of *personal and private* thoughts about God, The Church, you, your marriage and family, relationships, or your work and career. Though you may choose to discuss them with trusted friends, they may also be matters you will keep only for yourself and God. As long as these thoughts don't cross the boundaries of Eternal Life issues, continue to think and pray about them in the privacy of your intimate relationship with Jesus. In fact, you may be

---

[76] Romans 13:8 NLT

encouraged by meditating on Romans 14–15:13. You may find some instruction, encouragement, or clarity for both your Backyard and Closet Doctrine thinking.

This is Closet Doctrine
All matters of personal conscience and freedom
All matters for which there may be no clear Biblical instruction.
All those thoughts and issues for which you haven't yet discovered what
God thinks about it!

As I mentioned at the beginning of this chapter, this is a possible model that you and your family or local church may consider to assist you to experience the unity of the faith. Whether you agree with this model, its levels, or the distributions within the levels, really isn't as important as recognizing that the unity of the faith is within our reach if we are willing to lay down our lives for one another. This model also assists us to recognize that the majority of the disharmony in the body of Christ has been and is more about matters of personal preference and strong personal opinions! Church and denominational splits, people leaving churches, and various divisions and separations, in large measure, have not been about the essentials of Eternal Life doctrines. Frankly, they have more than likely, been about our flesh! My hope is this model will offer a place to begin your pursuit of intentional unity.

GOD'S PASSIONATE DESIRE... for unity in the church!

I remain committed to the unity of the body of Christ. Though I do not have a large platform, I do have a small sphere of influence in which I endeavor to be a catalyst for unity in The Church, in my marriage, family, personal relationships, and local community. The simple principle I live in is, if the issue at hand is not, in some way, related to Eternal Life doctrine, then the solution can be found in godly compromise. Imagine the impact of this in your life. Our love for Jesus and one another will increase, while our stress levels and frustrations with the saints will be greatly diminished. When we extrapolate this principle of unity into our ever-widening spheres of influence, we will see clearly just how effective satan has been keeping us focused on not loving one another rather than focusing on loving God. Personal and intentional unity with Jesus, will set us on the path to the corporate unity for which Jesus so passionately prayed.

CHAPTER SIX

INTENTIONAL UNITY

"Love is patient and kind. Love is not jealous or boastful or proud or rude. It does not demand its own way. It is not irritable, and it keeps no record of being wronged. It does not rejoice about injustice but rejoices whenever the truth wins out. Love never gives up, never loses faith, is always hopeful, and endures through every circumstance. But love will last forever."
I Corinthians 13:4–8b NLT

"If anyone claims, "I am living in the light," but hates a Christian brother or sister, that person is still living in darkness. Anyone who loves another brother or sister is living in the light and does not cause others to stumble.
I John 2:9–10 NLT

> "This is the message you have heard from the beginning: We should love one another. Dear children, let's not merely say that we love each other; let us show the truth by our actions."
> I John 3:11, 18 NLT

Unity is not a lesson to learn for sharing with others. Unity is not an intermittent series of unity opportunities to display my unity knowledge and skills. No! Intentional unity is the lifestyle of the Christian who, when he claims love and unity in Christ Jesus ". . . he shows the truth by his actions."[77] In fact, it is a divine impossibility to ". . . love the Lord your God with all your heart, all your soul, and all your mind . . . and your neighbor as yourself . . ."[78] and knowingly choose to live your life in disunity with anyone; especially a fellow believer. You have the choice to live in unity or disunity with God and man, but you cannot separate them and choose to love God but not your neighbor. There is no such thing as being partially obedient to Jesus and His Word. More than being silly and ludicrous, it is egregiously sinful. Our God is intolerant with the believer who deliberately chooses to ignore His instructions.

In the late 1980s my flesh-man wrestled with God for almost eighteen months. Since the early days of ministry my flesh desired the big-time ministry platforms. I carefully developed my opportunities while I led our church to be large

---

[77] 1John 3:18–19 NLT
[78] Matthew 22:37–39 NLT

INTENTIONAL UNITY

enough that our leaders and I were looking at twenty acre parcels of land in a more desirable area. A large and successful suburban ministry was waiting to happen. At the same time the Holy Spirit was pulling on my spirit to establish our growing ministry in an all–African-American neighborhood in the city of Detroit. I reasoned and wrestled with God in the secret places of my soul and spirit. I told no one—not even my wife. This was going to derail my dream. I knew it in my spirit.

This is when I learned the agony of choice comes before the promise of change. One day, as I was trying to concentrate on the available property's report our administrator was showing to me, the Lord spoke and said I had to choose. Was I going to move our all-white suburban congregation to the city, to become a catalyst for racial and cross denominational reconciliation, or was I going to follow my dream? I hesitated, and He said, "this is your choice. I will give you all you have dreamed, but I will send leanness to your soul[79] and spiritual mediocrity to your ministry, or you can follow Me." In my heart I knew there was only one choice! I wanted both my dream and obedience to Him. Much as it was in Abraham's choice regarding sacrificing Isaac, obedience was the only choice. Neither halfway or half-hearted is acceptable to Him.

Walking with Jesus is a lifestyle of intentional choices to please Him. Frankly, my spirit-man agonizes over the fashionably acceptable trend in the lives of too many Christians. Recently my wife and I were in church when the worship

---

[79] Psalm 106:15 NAS

leader began to lead one of the older songs, "I'm coming back to the heart of Jesus, and it's all about You, it's all about You, Jesus." As the congregation continued, I found myself singing, "I'm coming back to heart of me, and it's all about me, it's all about me, Jesus." It was the Spirit of God giving me a clear picture of a large percentage of The Church. Bound by mixture, half God and half self, The Church is becoming marginalized and therefore, neutralized. Thank the Lord for those occasional "hot pockets" of revival fires scattered across the country. It seems the trend is toward mixture—me and Jesus, rather than "the simplicity and purity of devotion to Jesus,"[80] which is intentional unity! There should be no mixture, because there is no satisfaction in a half-hearted commitment to Him. My choice to be obedient to the Lord was indeed a decision that expressed intentional unity. However, we quickly learned not everyone thought my choice was such a good idea, even if God did design it. Resistance was experienced from our church members and from the black pastors I met. Two hundred seventy-five people left the church in the first six months. Another one hundred dwindled away over the next year. That first year I shared our story with black leaders across the city. Regardless of how I told the story, or who I shared it with—large and famous or storefront—friendly, encouraging, helpful, and blessed were not the feelings I experienced. I finally met a few black pastors who became my brothers and friends. Those friendships continue to this day. The rich deposit of their lives opened doors to so

---

[80] 2 Corinthians 11:3 NLT

INTENTIONAL UNITY

many intentional unity opportunities for both of us. Until we left the city almost fifteen years later, they mentored me in cross-cultural relationships and ministry. Because racism is so prevalent in The Church today I want to address this issue in the light of intentional unity.

For more than ten years, in the circle of black leaders I originally met, it seemed all I heard were evidential stories of "the struggle" with the white man. From the day I met my brothers, it seemed all I heard were evidential stories of the powerful work of God in their lives and ministry. Now, it isn't that all these people weren't also in "the struggle." They were. When asked, they shared their families' stories. My point here is "the struggle" was, and obviously still is, very real. However, there is no excuse among born-again Christians for resistance, suspicion, and distrust to exist between us. It's all in our perspective on "the struggle" between the black and white races. Actually, our perspective is determined by the foundation for that perspective. Our view of this racial "war" is determined by our own flesh. The difference in our viewpoint is the motive of our heart. The view from the Spirit-man is focused on God's desires, and the view from the flesh-man is focused on me and my desires. The first acknowledges God is right and if there is anything that needs to be changed, it is me. The second expects that you can see you are the problem and therefore, it is your responsibility to initiate the changes necessary. Therefore, if we are ever going to come close to the unity of The Church, you have to make the next move. The Word and God are culturally and ethnically blind. The only person who should be waiting for someone to make the next move is God. He already made the first one. The flesh man, whoever he/she is, must die to sin, self, and the past. I submit that when you are born of the Spirit, you no longer have a past to blame. No, you have a future in Christ Jesus, filled with opportunities to be a catalyst for unity in The Church. These things apply to any conflict between believers, whether they are racial issues or not.

When we are born again of the Holy Spirit, we receive the divine nature of Jesus Christ.[81] We exchange our nationality for our new "citizenship in heaven."[82] In addition, we exchange our worldly culture for the culture of the Kingdom, *"on earth as it is in heaven."*[83] The only thing of our flesh God leaves unchanged is our ethnicity because He is demonstrating we are all the same in the realm of the Spirit. What is our problem, then? Quite bluntly, it is the flesh! Your color, ethnicity, economic status, education, previous treatment, and so on are not the issue. Your commitment to obey Jesus and His Word is. This is not to diminish the seriousness or the reality of some issues. They are real. We have sinned against one another drastically and it must be repented of and forgiveness must be gladly given. However, these issues can only live and be a problem as long as my flesh controls me. "Don't you realize that you become the slave of whatever you choose to obey?"[84] It doesn't matter what you loudly declare

---

[81] 2 Peter 1:3–4 NLT
[82] Ephesians 2:19 NLT
[83] Matthew 6:10 NLT
[84] Romans 6:15–18 (esp. v. 16) NLT

INTENTIONAL UNITY

publicly about how much we love one another. Our love is only as valid as the sacrifice *you* make for the well-being of one another.

Deliberate and intentional acts of unity are essential to a powerful verbal and visible expression of unity in The Church. Intentional unity under the most difficult of circumstances demonstrates the living reality "that we are mature in the Lord, measuring up to the full standard of Christ.[85] Though we tend to resist truth, most Christians know the one thing that makes a struggle last so long is our own unwillingness to yield to God and handle the struggle His way. In fact, the evidence He is looking for to demonstrate His Church has become mature is that it will pay any price to achieve that unity. It is the expression of maturity, and maturity is evidence that His Church has come into unity. The price we must pay is the same price Jesus paid on the cross, intentionally sacrificing our lives.

From the founding of The Church to the final preparation for the return of Jesus, the Holy Spirit inspired the New Testament writers to address unity in The Church over 120 times. Unity was the lifestyle of the first church until the early Jesus followers like The Church today had a better way. To indicate how personally He felt their disobedience and disruption of His unity desire, the Holy Spirit dealt with them severely. Those 120 times the Holy Spirit spoke were constant reminders to maintain and sustain the unity of The Church to the end.

---

[85] Ephesians 4:13 NLT

As I mentioned earlier, the practical outworking of that is found in being personally responsible to keep our relationship with Jesus strong and life-giving. My father often reminded us to "keep short accounts with Jesus." Restoring daily unity with Him releases within us the empowering desire to maintain our unity with our fellow believers. Love is strengthened in the atmosphere of unity, while unity contagiously affects the people because of the peace of God flowing out of you like a river of living water. Unity in The Church is attainable with Christians who are also passionate about unity. It is our imperative!

The passionate mandate for unity in The Church requires us to stop waiting for "somebody to do something about it." That somebody is you! It is time for you to be intentional in your home and in your church. Talk about it with your Christian friends; work together to intentionally build unity between you. Together, do something for your unbelieving friends. Let them experience the atmosphere of the Presence of the Spirit of unity when they are around you. Watch, as God uses your sphere of unified influence to attract friends and family to the love of God as it is demonstrated by your love and unity. To God, the unity of the church is not an option—it is His divine IMPERATIVE!

EPILOGUE

"Don't just pretend to love others. Really love them. Hate what is wrong. Hold tightly to what is good. Love each other with genuine affection, and take delight in honoring each other. Never be lazy, but work hard and serve the Lord, enthusiastically. Rejoice in our confident hope. Be patient in trouble, and keep on praying. when God's people are in need, be ready to help them. Always be eager to practice hospitality. Bless those who persecute you. Don't curse them; Pray that God will bless them.
Romans 12:9–14 NLT

One year ago I was prompted by God to write this little book. The unity of The Church has been the passion of my heart for many years. I thought this should be a fun project, and fairly easy to write. A few weeks later, I had a cardiac event that required a stent to be inserted to my main heart artery, which would prevent any future event. I have never been an unhealthy person. The Lord has been my gracious healer all my life, but there I was, recuperating. It took six weeks to get back to normal. O.K., I thought. Now let's get busy and do this. It will probably take six months. I experienced four more delays.

I wrote two complete drafts. As I wrote each one, the Lord challenged me with two issues that reappeared a few times. One issue was that He challenged my integrity often. I would hear, "You can't write that because you aren't walking in that yourself." Sometimes the delay was as long as a month while I got my heart pure before Him. The other issue, also an issue with my flesh-man, was that He would ask, "Why are you telling that story that way?" resulting in more delay while I allowed the purifying fire to cleanse my heart. The cleansing fire purifies the flesh, while it breaks the will. My greatest disappointment was that my Father still had so much purifying work to do in me.

The final delay came late in the summer. I experienced a hemorrhagic stroke that temporarily impaired my vision and left me a little wobbly, physically and emotionally. Another eight weeks were lost.

My wife has written this book with me. By that I mean

EPILOGUE

that she has experienced every painful dealing of God, every frustration of my heart, every victory, and every disappointment. She has seen and heard me weep with the joy of the Lord, and with the sadness of heart that His glorious church is not so glorious right now!

You have read the fourth and final draft. The first three drafts were much longer and filled with me. Neither God nor I liked them. This one is shorter with, I hope, more of Him and His passion in evidence.

As I mentioned, this has been a life-changing experience. Even if God wanted me to write it for my sake only, it has been worth the delays and disappointments. I have been additionally transformed, spirit, soul, and body, for which I am so thankful.

One final thing. Through the writing of this little book, I repeatedly asked myself,

"Am I really willing to pay the price, and make sacrifices necessary to ultimately experience the unity of The Church? Will my love for Jesus and His passionate desire remain strong to the end? O Lord Jesus, I long for that to be so."

> "I will bless those who have humble
> and contrite hearts, who tremble at
> My word."
> Isaiah 66:2 NLT

*How wonderful it is, how pleasant,
when brothers live together in harmony!
For harmony is as precious as the
fragrant anointing oil that was poured
over Aaron's head, that ran down his
beard and onto the border of his robe
Harmony is as refreshing as the dew from
Mount Hermon that falls on the
mountains of Zion.
And the Lord has pronounced his blessing,
even life forevermore.*

Psalm 133:1–3

Paul Bersche preaches, speaks, writes, and teaches as if his simple, transparent, and direct presentation of the Word is all the Holy Spirit needs to get us to see as God sees. Pastor Paul also believes that God's Word is the foundation for solutions to the whole wide variety of problems and battles in the Church and society!

Additional books by Paul Bersche

Is There a Father in the House?
Preparing spiritual sons to lead the Church

Victors . . . Not Victims
A revelation for spiritual warfare

A Primer on Apostolic Ministry Today
A description, in simple terms, of the ministry of a present day Apostle

To order books or to arrange for speaking engagements please contact:

Paul Bersche Ministries.com